let us play
I SPY
animals!

i spy play books by
© Little Dezign Press

ready to play
i spy animals?

just like real i spy game, letters are
not in alphabetical order.

i spy with my little
eye, something beginning with...

f is for...

FOX!

i spy with my little
eye, something beginning with...

P is for...

Pig!

i spy with my little eye, something beginning with...

C is for...

COW!

i spy with my little
eye, something beginning with...

g is for... giraffe!

i spy with my little
eye, something beginning with...

h is for...

horse!

i spy with my little
eye, something beginning with...

t is for...

tiger!

i spy with my little
eye, something beginning with...

d is for...
dog!

i spy with my little eye, something beginning with...

P is for...
penguin!

i spy with my little
eye, something beginning with...

e is for...

elephant!

i spy with my little

eye, something beginning with...

M is for... monkey!

i spy with my little eye, something beginning with...

C is for...

camel!

i spy with my little

eye, something beginning with...

Z is for...

zebra!

i spy with my little eye, something beginning with...

K

K is for...

kangaroo!

i spy with my little
eye, something beginning with...

C is for...

cat!

i spy with my little
eye, something beginning with...

g is for...
goat!

i spy with my little
eye, something beginning with...

S

S is for...
snake!

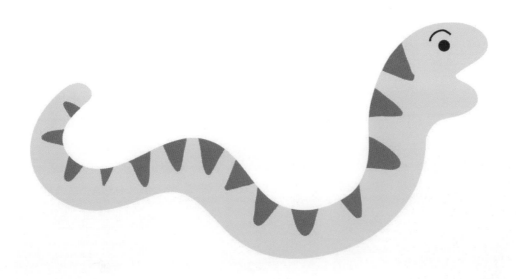

i spy with my little eye, something beginning with...

r is for...

raccoon!

i spy with my little
eye, something beginning with...

l is for...

lion!

i spy with my little
eye, something beginning with...

O

O is for...

OWL!

Printed in Poland
by Amazon Fulfillment
Poland Sp. z o.o., Wrocław

64039488R00026